Getting the Hell out of Here.

or

What happens after you die?

Getting the Hell out of Here.

or

What happens after you die?

Author: Geoffrey John Cutler.

The front cover image is © Bcubic - Fotolia.com, and the image on the back cover is © jeancliclac - Fotolia.com. Permission to quote the work of the medium HR of Cuenca, Ecuador is gratefully acknowledged.

ISBN: 978-1-4475-5744-9

GETTING THE HELL OUT OF HERE.

OR

WHAT HAPPENS AFTER YOU DIE?

FOREWORD.

I could not resist picking a cute non-boring title. I trust I did not upset anyone right up front! I decided to write this booklet so that I have something available that is comprehensive yet relatively simple when dealing with folks who are interested in hearing about the next world – our eternal destination. And as I age, naturally I meet more and more folk who have lost a dear one. This is often the stimulus to ask:

"What happens after death?"

It is my objective to try and write something that is largely devoid of undue moralizing, or religious framework. I initially decided to leave out the sources of my findings, but in this latest revision I have decided to add a list of the more significant sources. This will allow someone who would like to review this summary, and obtain greater insight, to do so. I have read very widely on this subject, and this now summarises some ten years of research. There are sometimes great differences of opinion out there. That does not mean I am right, but I will have good reasons why I believe what I believe.

Where does all this stuff come from? The other side of course! And of course, none of us has "proof." The fact that I believe I spent thirty minutes talking to my deceased mother does not constitute scientific proof. Although the comments she directed to me, that referred to one-way thought conversations I had had with her, pretty well convinced me. That fact, as far as science is concerned, is limited to my spending 30 minutes in the company of a dear friend who is a trance medium. Even the bit about trance medium is not accepted by science, although just recently they have found that some people can know things about total strangers that is way beyond statistical chance. Incidentally, my mother contributed virtually nothing to this paper, as she was still too new in spirit to know what is going on. But proof to me is finding two or more credible sources with the same issue described. Credible does not to me necessarily mean entirely accurate. Spirits just like humans have opinions, and do not all agree amongst themselves. But a spirit looking down from a substantial spiritual height is likely to be more accurate than one new to spirit life. I am also always more impressed by actual spirit experiences, than their opinions about something that may happen in their future.

I would like to add a caveat. If you were to pick 100 locations across this earth, and then take the description of one single example as a perfect example of life on earth, clearly there are going to be many who would have significantly different experiences to that one sample of earth life. So too are life after death stories. Expect differences in the experience that every person will have, but if you look for similarities, these you will find. Now that this document has been revised over an eight year period, it is becoming difficult to keep short and to the point. In fact the more you learn, the more you realize that life after death is even more complex than life here. So I apologize in advance to any reader who is aware that some things have been simplified.

You may wonder why reincarnation is not even mentioned in this booklet. That is because it is, in my opinion, an illusion. If you would like more information on my research there, look for my publication[1] on that subject.

Geoff Cutler.

---

[1] Is Reincarnation an Illusion?

Table of Contents

Getting the Hell out of Here

DEATH.

I guess the first question to ask is whether we all survive death? Until recently I would not have had any doubt about that, but it seems there is a small complication for some people. Many people would be aware that the universe appears to attempt to supply that which we focus on, even if it is not good for us. Those people who are adamant that there is no life after death, and make this a certainty in their life often do not pass immediately from one realm to the next in a conscious state. They are termed "sleeping survivors."[2] These folks almost get their most fervent wish - annihilation. They may sleep for centuries, before a group awakening. More recent information now suggests that relatively few pass over as "Sleeping Survivors" at the present time. This may be because the rules have been changed, as we enter the "Correcting Time" and also possibly because there are far more Celestial helpers available at this time. I assume these "tough cases" were grouped together as an efficiency measure which enabled them to handle these folks en-mass.[3]

But the majority of us simply pass from one state to another, with very little lost time. Some reports state three days are lost in this transition, but I now believe that is probably incorrect, and may simply be an attempt to insert some Biblical material. Depending on your physical health as you depart this life, you may be instantly conscious of your existence in the next realm, or require some healing in the next. Thus you may pass almost without any break in consciousness. Obviously one would not be aware of lost time, so this issue is impossible to

---

[2] The Urantia Book mentions these on page 340.

3 A wonderful example is contained in Letter 38 in "Letters from the Light" published by Beyond Words Publishing and based on the out of print publication "Letters from a living dead man" where it is Letter 39.

answer accurately without third party feedback. However there are many stories which suggest almost no break in "time" occurs.

If you are awake, there is no knowing quite how death will unfold. This is because as the brain shuts down, you can experience many different effects. Most of these are anything but spiritual, although you might think that they do feel spiritual. They are simply the results of the brain shutting down. You might have a "life review", sort of like a movie. You may see white tunnels, or black tunnels. You might even have an instant out of body experience, where you are floating above your body, looking down on the scene, and that certainly is a spiritual event. Sometimes if the physical body is about to be badly damaged, the spirit body is withdrawn before impact or injury. This gives rise to the out of body experience, where you look down as an outsider on your own body, and will avoid you feeling any pain.

If you are consciously expecting death, things are probably going to be a bit different. Many people know that they are dying, and seem to gain additional abilities or insights in the last hours or days. They often start to see their spirit guides, and may feel the presence of their love, and be quite calm. There is no reason to panic. For one it is not going to help, and secondly, for the vast majority of us, what follows is a big improvement over life on earth. The spirit folks who are full time workers assisting us to pass over will be in attendance at your passing. Generally this job is left entirely to these skilled beings, and your spirit family generally waits until you are settled, and then arrives to welcome you. If you are weakening in the last hours of life, you most likely may see one or two of these spirit beings who assist, as this will limit any concern when you see them from the other side.

You might be met by dear loved ones who passed over before you, but it is more likely it will be one of those tasked with this function. As you pass through death, initially they may be seen only as a bright white light. This is the basis of the reported white tunnel. Some folks have reported meeting Jesus, (if Christian!) but this is very unlikely to happen. Not that he is not around, but if he was there, you almost certainly would not recognize him – unless you already know what he looks like – and more to the point he has far more important things to be doing. Might he have welcomed Mother Teresa? I think that is very likely, but I do not know that for a fact, but I do know of another individual he did welcome. Take it from me, you need to have been doing a pretty special job on earth to warrant that compliment. And the chances are that you would not need to be reading this book, if that is true. But the folks who assist with this transition know what they are doing, and some of them could appear like a very advanced spirit being. But generally they try to appear as non-threatening as possible and adjust their clothing to suit the occasion.

However it seems that those who see the "tunnel of light" or actually recognize some of the beings, who are there to meet the newly departed, are in the minority. Far too many depart this life with inadequate spiritual preparation, and the result is that they have great difficulty in triggering their spiritual vision and spiritual hearing. You can imagine that moving from a situation where you operate out of a physical brain, even though it is linked to a spirit mind, is a very different situation when that physical brain is gone, and you must operate entirely with spirit faculties. The result is that many spend a period of time in a dazed state, in almost complete silence, and in almost total darkness. In the meantime, their "greeters" are frantically trying to make some sort of break through. So if it happens to you, and you hear music, or see shadows or faint voices, do make an effort to hear and see more clearly. The irony is that because the next realm is subject to the influence of our thoughts, simply believing and saying: "I can see" or "I can hear" will trigger the required spiritual vision and hearing.

You may notice that you are completely naked, but this is not often the case. Probably because almost immediately, your spirit companions will "create" spirit clothes for you. There are various opinions as to whether they wear diaphanous gowns, or clothes that you are familiar with. It seems that it varies, and varies particularly according to your station in the next realm. So the attendants may in fact change into our style of clothing for some hours to ease the transition and avoid scaring you. These spirit clothes are great. They don't get dirty and they don't wear out either. And you can change them just by thinking a new outfit, assuming you are sufficiently spiritually advanced. But as individuals progress, they seem to all adopt a sort of diaphanous gown which has very specific colours reflecting the development and even the personality of the individual.

The very first thing that is going to happen to you, as you begin to realize something strange is happening, is that you will travel. I have only a vague idea how far that is, and it will probably not take more than a few seconds, or maybe a few minutes. While a lot of people report going to a way station, each person can have a unique experience. So from this point on, it's very hard to say what will exactly happen to you. For example if you departed this earth life in need of significant spiritual repair, it's almost certain you will be taken unconscious to a hospital (albeit rather different to ours!) for recovery, and you would regain your consciousness in that location. This repair can cover emotional as well as physical weaknesses. Some people are in effect scarred by their life experiences and need considerable work before they are freed from these effects. Curiously the material and the physical worlds can be quite interwoven, to have outcomes in the spiritual realm that result from the physical.

Let's assume that you will arrive at a way station, a collection point for recently deceased individuals, as this is relatively common. No doubt with much coming and going. It is very pleasant, attractive, with a very loving atmosphere, and you will soon feel very relaxed. It has been described as a station concourse, but I don't think that describes a loving atmosphere, although it may well be accurate in terms of comings and goings, and meeting loved ones. Sometimes these places are described as outside, on a hillside. It will undoubtedly feel like the best place you have ever been to. Things are looking up, you conclude. When you arrive in the next realm you will immediately notice an up step in frequency, not just in your own spirit body but in your surroundings as well. What you begin to experience is a higher frequency in which you exist. The colours are more vibrant; the plant life is more lush and alive.

If at this point you start to think about what you have left behind, you might find that you are right back there. In other words, you can travel, virtually instantly, just by thinking about it. So you might well see your family back on earth, shedding tears about your passing. But they won't see you, or hear you. You are much better off at this stage going back to the transition place; particularly as at this very early stage you will still have strong earth attractions. Later on it is safer to travel back to earth because these ties will have dissipated. Back on "earth" you may be able to see everything just as you used to, but you will find that nothing is solid. You can pass through people, walls, everything. But the ability to discern things on earth seems to be inversely related to the degree of spiritual advancement of the individual, and is one of the faculties that can be lost quite quickly. So some people can see the earth and its human forms relatively clearly in this early stage if they are somewhat unevolved spiritually, while others have as much difficulty as we do in seeing spirit. However, you will notice that you can "hear" dear mortal friends thinking about you, and you may almost instantly visit them. If you are really lucky, you may find a few who can "feel" your presence, and this will give you a big thrill, just as it will give them a thrill to know you are around. You may even be able to create a few "signs" that let folk know you are still around. Things like leaving a telltale cigar smell, or making a noise or two, or leaving your favourite flower where it will be seen, or perhaps by leaving a scent in the air. How they do those things? [4]

But back at the way-station, things are very solid. You can hug old friends, and they can certainly "hear" you. The spirit body appears very solid, and still appears to need to breathe, but does not need sleep or

---

[4] A reader suggested I read "More Alive Than Ever... Always Karen" by Jeanne Walker. It is clear from this book that these physical effects are the result of thought forms created by the spirit from their realm.

food as sustenance. But, in the early phase, sleep may be required; however that phase will soon pass. While you can talk in the old conventional way, you will also discover that it seems to be possible to converse just via thoughts. Then you notice that they must be hearing your thoughts, and you hearing their thoughts. And then you have a dreadful realization – these folk know everything about you! They can simply read your memories. And they hear your thoughts! You recall that time you got Fred fired by making up a confidential report, and rather stretching the facts to suit, now here you have to look Fred in the eye. He knows, but strangely he's not mad. Or maybe, you remember wearing that really low cut dress for the Christmas party and how successful it was in starting that affair with Joe. And here is Sally, Joe's partner, smiling at you. Total openness leads to the rapid realization that all of us fail from time to time. Actually not all thoughts are shared, so we can still have some secrets!

During this period of orientation, you start to notice that not all spirits are quite the same. Some have a beautiful countenance and way about them. And they are brighter, and amazingly loving. This brightness seems to come right out of them. Others are baser, dark, indeed some are downright ugly. As you wonder why this might be, you suddenly begin to wonder where you fit in. Are you ugly, or beautiful? Bright or dark?

At this point you will also know that you are just the same person that you were in the mortal life. With the same beliefs, memories, attitudes, values, fears, unresolved issues and loves. How did this happen? After all, your brain is already consigned to dust. Quite simply, as a mortal on earth you had three major components. There was your soul, which as far as we can tell, was probably billions of years old. Then there was your spirit body, which encapsulates the soul, and takes on the appearance of the mortal body. Just as well, because none of us can see souls, but we can see spirit bodies. It seems that the spirit body is a sort of reflection of the enclosed soul. If this soul is pure, the spirit body is literally full of light. If the soul is tarnished, the spirit body is dark, even ugly. And finally of course you had a mortal body. While you may have thought that all your memories were in your brain, it seems it is not quite so. The spirit body houses the mind, and the brain is the transducer that allows the physical body to interact with the spirit body and its mind. So you may have lost the physical body, but most folks report feeling much lighter, and far prefer only having a spirit body. For one thing, it has no defects. If you lost a leg, you will find you are now perfect. If your brain suffered from senile dementia, you will have no such limitation now. And there are some neat tricks you will learn in the future in regards to your spirit body, as you progress spiritually. I have recently learnt that the spirit body itself is complex, and has at least two constituents, one being a relatively gross astral body, and the other a more etheric spirit body.

Just at this point, the spirits who manage this transition process, explain that in the heavens, the Law of Attraction is paramount. Every spirit has to live where it fits in – where it is in harmony. And, yes, those beautiful ones, that seem somehow ethereal, are more advanced, and no, most probably you won't live with them. You can look down at your hands, or ask for a "mirror" to see how you rate. They will explain that you can progress beyond where you start out, but probably you won't be listening closely enough. You may be concerned that you are not going to be living with your dear Madge, who passed some years before you. She says that she will come and visit you regularly. Things are rapidly beginning to sound more complicated.

THE STRUCTURE OF THE HEAVENS.

I guess many practical folk have long realized you can get almost no sense out of most religions when you ask about heaven. All that singing and harp plucking stuff that is supposed to go on, and strutting around on streets of gold. Or maybe the idea that you are going to be asleep until some great day of judgment. And particularly the notion that you will be magically, and instantly "perfect".

It is far more logical to consider that since mortals have been around a very long time, probably over a million years on earth, that there has been a heaven all that time, with spirits in it. Certainly the holy books, like the Bible, happily report interactions with the spirit world going back many years before Jesus. Perhaps I should point out here, that the spirit realm that I am about to discuss would appear not to be the **Kingdom of God** that so many orthodox Christians expect to enter via Jesus' help. This is undoubtedly the cause of a great deal of confusion, and even heartache. It is what has led so many Christians to conclude, incorrectly, that only they will get to "heaven" and everyone else will only get to "hell." The real issue is "which" heaven, something they have not considered, even though a significant clue is given in the Bible that there may be more than one "heaven", in a reference to the "third heaven" in the New Testament.[5] The main part of this paper covers the **Kingdom of Spirit**, also called the Spirit Spheres and not the **Kingdom of God**.

It may even be the case that we create this spirit heaven ourselves. Not to suggest God has nothing to do with it, but as spirits we have great powers, which powers increase as the spirit advances. So it would not

---

[5] **2 Corinthians 12:2**: I know a man in Christ who fourteen years ago was caught up to the third heaven. Whether it was in the body or out of the body I do not know—God knows.

surprise me if in fact the "realities" that are found are created by the spirits that are there. And this creation need not necessarily be conscious. This would explain why some spirits, and indeed many NDE's, (Near Death Experiences) seem to describe confusingly different places. We have explanations of Jewish heavens, and the classic Christian heavens, complete with harps, witnessing and bright holy images. We have descriptions of fire and brimstone hells, and also dark places that are simply cold, sad, dead places. One thing that is quite clear, the belief system of the spirit has a very large effect on the experience it will have. Whether this is only a function of the Law of Attraction, which causes like-minded spirits to congregate, or whether it is the will of the spirit that creates a "reality" it expects, is uncertain. But what is certain, is that real places exist, that vary substantially.

The most common description of the Kingdom of Spirit talks about seven "spheres" or "worlds". However these should not be taken too literally. But it seems that however they are constructed, they are immense in size. There is absolutely no shortage of space.

Then there are also the vast uncountable heavens beyond the Seventh Sphere. Where are all these places? Well, we are not sure, but the universe is very much larger than man has supposed. Apparently what we humans think is the entire universe is but a very tiny corner of one of many super universes.[6] And some 80% of the material is apparently not visible to man anyway, but is visible to spirit. Could it be another dimension? It almost certainly is, because the First Spirit Sphere is located right here, somewhere in the space created by our orbit round the sun. That is extremely large, and obviously very close. But irrespective of the number of time/space dimensions that may exist, the distances involved in traversing our Universe are immense. Added to this, the solid material of the next realm can co-exist in space with solid material from our realm. So different solid objects can occupy the same spot, one in each dimension.

---

[6] The Urantia Book

One of the difficulties or problems in getting a good description of the heavens comes from the apparent fact that the bottom up view is so limited and confused. Folks enter at the bottom of this schema, with very limited knowledge, and so they have to learn a great deal, over many years, before they could really be considered to know. And even then, as we will see later, time in spirit does not equate to advancement.

We are accustomed, on earth, to always know who is in charge, and how things are organized. But in the next realm free will is paramount. You will not be used to this idea, as earth is quite different. If you want to believe something, you will be allowed to believe that, and furthermore, the Law of Attraction will ensure that you find yourself amongst others of like mind, who will agree with your outlook. So, you will be in the situation that unless you ask for information, you will be left with your belief. It is not going to happen that someone will knock at your door, proselytize and hand out a few pamphlets. That might be a relief for quite a few of us! Even the issue of religious groups is interesting. There are still many folks in spirit that insist on following their old earth based religion. However they are absolutely not allowed to proselytize.

There is another problem. Spirits are confined, to a large degree, to the sphere in which they reside. This is where they are in harmony, and they would not feel comfortable any higher or lower in the scheme. This does not mean that all in the same sphere are identical in outlook. One can still find intellectuals and religious folk in the same sphere, but typically not in close proximity. Indeed there are many such diverse groupings, called planes, within each sphere.

There is also the issue that your perception is a function of your spiritual development. So, if you are in the First sphere, you may be told there are other spheres, but you may not be able to see them. This is not like living in Australia, and knowing that there are other continents, such as the Americas, and knowing you could live there if you wanted to, or go there for an extended holiday. It is possible to have a very short visit to a higher sphere, but to achieve this you need to be taken there by someone with the spiritual power to enable you to travel there. What I am sure of is that you will find Catholics living together, groups of intellectuals, Muslims, Jews, Buddhists etc. And each of these groups will believe that their current happiness is a function of what they believe. This is not surprising, except if they compared themselves carefully with others, this would immediately illustrate the falsity of the idea. In this sense I describe things as confused from the bottom up.

A great many other folks have simply given up their earth based religious beliefs. In fact in the list of sources are a few books by Monsignor Robert Hugh Benson (received by Antony Borgia[7]) who although a Roman Catholic cleric, gave up all his prior religious beliefs inside a few hours. Such is the reality of the next realm, that many of peoples' earth beliefs simply cannot withstand the reality. And I suspect that the rest who cling to outdated beliefs, as though it is a sort of security blanket, simply because it is what they are used to. And in yet others, it is because they don't know what else to believe. Indeed modern statistics will tell us only a small percentage of us are "early adopters" – people who are happy to try new things and are actively out there looking for new experiences.

There is no overall agreement about what happens next, and what is best for spiritual progression or what is the "right" belief. In fact I don't even think these lower spirits generally know who is in charge, and maybe some are only vaguely aware of the desirability of seeking to progress. So I would guess there may be spirits in the First Sphere who might dispute that there is a Second Sphere, never mind an almost unlimited number beyond that!

Those "in charge" always respect the free will choices of these spirits, so it is only through a conscious choice to follow a leader's direction, that people can be said to be led. The leaders are far more advanced,

---

[7] *"Life in the World Unseen"*, by Anthony Borgia

live somewhere else where you cannot go, and cannot be seen unless they decide to make themselves visible. This is because the more advanced spirits have an ability to conceal themselves from less advanced spirits. In some ways it is like it is on earth when we try to understand what happens after death. Our perception of the next realm is limited, and indeed there are many on earth that would dispute that there is any life after death.

The authority that we were used to on earth is simply absent. In that sense you can experience total freedom of choice to do as you please. Whether that might be doing something, or doing almost nothing. But it also means you can follow dozens of spiritual paths that don't lead anywhere special. In fact almost everything that you do will probably lead to increased happiness, so it is very easy to believe you are on the "right" path. And this is typically how spirits continue. They ascribe their current happiness to the path they are on, but it may be that there is nothing special about that path compared to many other paths.

However in another respect the spheres are supremely organized, with no chaos or poor organization. There is always someone in charge of a specific function, and they love their job, and have been superbly trained to perform it perfectly. So if you feel like being trained in a specific activity, this can be accomplished perfectly.

Of course there are other things that make it easy. You don't need to eat, although folks apparently enjoy nuts and fruits in the Spirit Spheres. They don't have digestive organs, so these foods are not eaten as we do on earth, but apparently more like "inhaled." The same with water, this refreshes, but is not used to sustain. Since you don't need to eat, clearly you don't need a job to earn money to survive. Indeed there is no money, because all you need is given. So, you will do things because you enjoy them, not because you have to. Well, that depends on where you are. These comments would appear to not apply in the lowest planes of the First Sphere that we will talk about soon.

Although we describe the Spirit Heavens as having seven spheres, in reality there are an almost infinite number of "planes" within these. In a sense, one's spirituality acts like a sort of gravity. The less spiritual you are, the further down you will sink, possibly right to the bottom. And the bottom is called hell. In fact, the really advanced spirits consider that all of the first and Second Spheres contain some darkness. But, for us earthlings, anything from the top of the First Sphere upwards is just great. There are in fact three portions of the First Sphere that could almost be called separate spheres, and seem to be numbered separately by Spiritualists. They typically also name them such as Twilight Lands, Dawn Lands and Summerland. But before we talk about these dark places, we will discuss the Astral Plane.

THE ASTRAL PLANE.

The Astral Plane is a grosser dimension than the Spirit Spheres, and is a physicality just as the Spirit Spheres are. Very little has been received about this plane, and that is yet another reason why some reports about life after death appear to contradict each other – the Spiritual Laws here are different to those in the Spirit Spheres. Some spirits seem not to know that they are in the Astral Plane, and this is the home of earth bound entities. The term "earth bound" is given by spiritualists to spirits that are here around the earth, and they often try to convince them to "pass over".

There are higher levels and lower levels of the Astral Plane, and it exists both above and below the surface of the Earth. The Earth Plane is the third of the seven divisions of the Astral Plane. However, in order to reach the Spirit Spheres proper, we have to discard both our physical bodies, and another body called an astral body. People who have out of body experiences, can travel in the astral, using their astral body, or leave the astral body and the physical body, and travel in the spirit spheres with their spirit body. It seems the silver chord that is reported as joining us to our physical bodies while alive is a part of the astral body, so any reports of entities with silver chords indicates they are astral travelling. Some references to the Astral Plane simply use the word "Earth Plane" as the description, probably because the Astral Plane is in very close proximity to earth. In any event, one of the seven planes in the Astral is itself called the Earth Plane.

Although earlier I described the "passing over" after death to a special arrivals area for newly arrived spirits, there have been countless descriptions of others who did not even notice that they had died, so instantaneous was their transition. These folk, sometimes even thirty years after death still do not realize that they are dead. Very frequently their description is of passing from life to death virtually instantly, only that the room and mortals that were there pre-death suddenly become hard or impossible to see clearly. These events seem typical of passing to the Astral Plane, rather than the Spirit Spheres. Another difference, related to the Astral Plane, is spirits reporting that immediately after death that they are tied to something, which may last hours or days, although time is hard to discern, but during that period they may notice the funeral and burial. It appears that the astral body may take quite some time to separate from the physical body after death, and this gives the sensation of being tied to an invisible object. It is the silver chord which ties the astral body to the physical body which has not yet broken.

While I cannot be sure that the arrivals areas described earlier are all located in the Spirit Spheres, I currently believe that to be the case. The spirit can however only reach an arrivals hall if the recently deceased mortal is not still wearing their astral body. The older one is, the more likely that one's astral body will decay rapidly after death and release one for the Spirit Spheres. The same is true of those that are advanced spiritually. But those that die young have a very strong astral body, and they will often spend considerable time in the astral planes, of which there are seven, until they are able to cast off the astral body. The astral plane appears to give spirits who had very little earth time an opportunity to find their way spiritually. They can interact with both evil ex-mortals and spiritually advanced ex-mortals here, and they have an added ability that deception is not possible on this plane. However, if they are attracted to earthly pleasures, this desire will remain, and can prove their undoing. It also seems to be the case that accidental death may result in the spirit arriving in the Astral Plane. This seems to happen to soldiers in wartime, as an example. But it may be as much to do with their relative youth.

Those that fall into this category without exception have no understanding of what really happens after death. Many believe that the dead lie asleep till the "great resurrection." With that in mind, they conclude they can't be dead. Others don't even have that concept and just complain that they can no longer see because of the darkness. But later they recover their vision, and find a world that is very similar to earth, yet with differences.

Other spirits of a very material bent find themselves in the Earth plane. There seem to be many reasons for this. They may have had an unexpected bad experience, such as being murdered, and this may have left them with a desire for revenge. It seems the shock of a sudden death may indeed be a factor in how successfully one transitions. They may also be of limited spiritual development, but not necessarily bad. Another reason is a desire to look after a family, or even to try to enjoy, or protect material possessions. They may then hang around their last place of living, for a long period of time. Some are intensely religious, but of the mindless type. Yet they start out no better off than someone who never gave life after death a moment's thought.

In the Astral Plane, it is possible to eat and drink, and apparently the astral body will produce excreta. However there is no need for either and this is typical of the choices spirits face. If they indulge the desire for food and drink, this generally leads to a dark entity suggesting at some time that they can get a better experience by obsessing a living mortal. And since that carries a heavy spiritual penalty, eventually they pass into the hells. There are churches here too, but sadly they seem incapable of actually teaching anything more useful than that learned on earth, and many of the pastors are here, precisely because they are not spiritual.

There are also a class of entity which we often see as "ghosts", who are not actually earth bound spirits. Specifically in the case where a mortal has a lot of negative experiences, as might be if they were tortured, murdered, or otherwise badly treated, these experiences have to be resolved. And until they are resolved, which includes the individuals who caused the trauma, they may leave an energetic signature which behaves and looks like an earthbound. In fact these are simply astral shells, devoid of a soul, because the individual has moved into the spirit spheres, but this energetic bundle still may be tied to a location or another entity in darkness. It is very difficult from our side of the veil to know whether one is dealing with an astral shell sans soul, or a real spirit entity. These astral shells are dissipated only when the emotional issues surrounding them are resolved. There are some other entities in the Astral Plane, some of which are wonderful, and others which are dangerous. Provided that you have not distanced yourself from your guide, you will be protected, but if you have totally ignored spiritual matters, your guide will not be there to protect you, and the experience can be very unpleasant. While a spirit body can experience pain, and even be apparently damaged, it repairs itself rapidly, but it cannot be destroyed. The astral body will also repair itself normally, but as it is not eternal in nature, apparently it can be completely destroyed by some of the evil elementals, and this results in that (dark) spirit passing into the dark planes of the First Sphere – hell. This sort of thing can only happen in the lowest of the astral divisions, which are considered the anti-chamber of hell.

HELL.

Let's start by pointing out that the classic description of hell given by churches is very inaccurate. Fire and brimstone is not how things are. You will also find plenty of "new age" folk will deny there is any hell at all, no matter how it is constructed. They will tell you they have never had any feedback from the other side to suggest anything like it. They report that all spirits are loving and that there is only love. That may be so, mostly because very few spirits in hell are keen to admit this to loved ones on earth. It is also the case that folks who are able to astral travel, have reported that they cannot find a hell. That would be correct, since the Astral Plane does not contain hell. This is a part of the Spirit Spheres, and is not reachable if you are travelling in the astral.

Certainly there are not a great number of detailed reports[8] of life in the darkest spheres, but there are enough to satisfy a determined researcher. I have personally worked with people who were seriously troubled by dark spirits, and my mother has also told me my sister is (or was) in darkness. And, once you understand how the universe works, there has to be a place where those who are seriously out of harmony reside until they learn. It is just inconceivable that God would suddenly make loving spirits out of those who have chosen to be unloving. No, our progress is entirely dependent upon ourselves. That is what it means to be a free will creature. We must create ourselves and the result is our responsibility.

---

[8] James Padgett did receive a very great number of communications from folks in the hells, but I would not call these particularly detailed descriptions, although some are relatively detailed. Many of these can be found on the web here: www.new-birth.net/hell.htm

I have only found two books with an extensive treatment of the dark planes. These are "A Wanderer in the Spirit Lands" by Franchezzo and "Gone West" by J.S.M Ward.

What is it like in hell? Here is a description:

In this hell of mine, and there are many like it, instead of beautiful homes, as the other spirits described, we have dirty, rotten hovels all crooked and decayed, with all the foul smells of a charnel house ten times intensified, and instead of beautiful lawns and green meadows and leafy woods filled with musical birds making the echoes ring with their songs, we have barren wastes, and holes of darkness and gloom and the cries and cursings of spirits of damnation without hope; and instead of living, silvery waters we have stagnant pools filled with all kinds of repulsive reptiles and vermin, and smells of inexpressible, nauseating stinks.

I tell you that these are all real, and not creatures of the imagination or the outflowing of bitter recollections. And as for love, it has never shown its humanizing face in all the years that I have been here - only cursings and hatred and bitter scathings and imprecations, and grinning spirits with their witchlike cacklings. No rest, no hope, no kind words or ministering hand to wipe away the scalding tears which so often flow in mighty volumes. No, hell is real and hell is here.

We do not have any fire and brimstone, or grinning devils with pitch forks and hoofs and horns as the churches teach; but what is the need or necessity for such accompaniments? They would not add to the horrors or to our torments. I tell you my friend that I have faintly described our homes in these infernal regions and I cannot picture them as they are.

But the horror and pity of it all is that hope does not come to us with one faint smile to encourage us that there may at some time be an ending to all these torments, and in our hopeless despair we realize that our doom is fixed for all eternity.[9] (See a later explanation about the duration of hell.)

This is of course but one description, and as mentioned earlier, you should not be surprised to discover many variations on a theme. Some hells are places of isolation, others are cities of shared horrors, presided over by tyrannical rulers with very nasty temperaments, and stronger wills than their subjects.

Perhaps we should not use the word hell, because it is not a permanent situation, although commonly believed to be so by its inhabitants. There is no eternal damnation. In fact there is no damnation at all. Hell is simply a place where dreadful spirits live, until they choose not to be dreadful. So how long could you be there then? It all depends on you. How low in the hells you are, and how soon you start to try to get out. Yes but how long? From feedback, there are two ways out, the normal way, which is pretty slow, and the short cut way.

The normal way involves the spirit realizing that he/she is there because of their attitudes and values, and then deciding to change, and slowly changing, by being kind to his companions. If you were really bad on earth, you could expect this process to take longer than a lifetime, but it is often long because it may take the individual a very long time to discover that they are causing this unpleasant experience by virtue of their own behaviours. There is another curious thing about the hells that spirits trying to change seem to be more at the mercy of their compatriots than those who are not interested in change. The hells also seem to have well demarcated districts which are physically hard to exit; both in terms of finding a way out, and in getting past those that would prevent your exit. Generally it is only

---

[9] www.new-birth.net/tgrabjvol2/hell14.htm received by James Padgett, January 5th, 1916.

with the assistance of a substantially more developed spirit companion who is tasked with this job that anyone gets out.

Some historically bad spirits, like the Roman Emperors, seem to have spent up to a thousand years in darkness. Julius Caesar was still in hell in 1915, but got out with some help, in 17 months.[10] That means he had been in hell for 2040 years, a very long time indeed. Judas also learnt of the short cut, naturally from the apostles. Apparently Andrew and Mary Magdalene were always close to Judas, and they encouraged him to apply the knowledge that Jesus had taught them. Judas had not really understood these spiritual teachings, and in fact neither did the Apostles till after Jesus had departed. A more recent example is Neville Chamberlain,[11] whose appeasement policies effectively aided the Nazi regime, and is still paying the price, although he died in 1940.

The first thought that probably you might have, if you end up here, is that you did not appear to have a big day of judgment. You did not end up in front of God, and get judged. In fact, judgment happened every day and every second of your mortal life. When you broke a Spiritual Law, your soul was encrusted immediately, and that was that. Now you have to in effect clean your soul yourself. You could have done that on earth, if you had chosen to, but it did not seem to affect your material life having an encrusted soul. Well I might debate how much real happiness and peace you felt on earth with a heavily encrusted soul, but you can retort that it did not affect starting the Ferrari. Or distributing illicit drugs, whatever took your fancy.

So how bad is hell really? It depends. Frankly, the upper reaches of "hell" would be better than many folk's experience of life on earth. The darkest depths are not good however. Here it is reported one can be in total darkness, unable to perceive anyone or anything, totally alone

---

[10] www.new-birth.net/tgrabjvol3/minor274.htm received by James Padgett May 1st 1917.

[11] www.new-birth.net/contemporary/fab539.htm received by the medium FAB January 1st, 2011.

with only your own thoughts and memories. Many spirits report that they would choose annihilation, if it were an option. The emotional darkness and irritations and attentions of the other dark spirits make it a very unpleasant experience. It also appears that in the lowest of levels, the spirit bodies are very dense, and deformed. They appear to be affected by things like thirst and fire, even though these things do not affect more advanced spirits. It also appears possible to inflict physical damage on a spirit body, at the lowest levels, so that they do suffer injury and pain. And because the spirit body repairs itself very quickly, this pain can be repeated over and over again. The ability to move above the surface seems absent because these dark spirits are so gross. So they can be trapped in physical obstacles like swamps or holes, or have to physically ascend cliffs and mountains while trying to get out of some divisions.

What are my chances of ending up there? If you are a normal person, neither particularly good, nor particularly bad, then you will probably land up at the top of the first sphere. It could be a bit lower, or possibly a bit higher. You might not ever realize that this is "hell", and just think life after death is simply nowhere near what you had expected. On the other hand, if you were a poor African, or Asian, eking out a tough existence on earth, battling disease and hunger, trying to keep your children safe and alive, you may think this "hell" is a huge improvement over your earth experiences. If you have really tried on earth, and consider that you adhered strictly to your religious beliefs, and more particularly those relating to living in love, and caring for your fellows, which basically all religions espouse, you might make the Second Sphere, or higher. But statistically, the "normal" result is the first sphere.

So how do you get out of darkness? Actually help is always available, although right at the bottom, it may take some time before that help can be perceived. The problem is that most spirits in darkness are too embarrassed to even acknowledge the help offered to them. We are none of us an island, and thus everyone knows someone, and so it's almost always the case that there is someone who you know, who is more advanced, and who you could therefore trust. The more advanced spirits are always trying to help those that are less developed, even in darkness, particularly if there is a personal relationship. But their advances are most often rebuffed. So the first lesson is to be prepared to ask for, and accept help. The spirits that can help are those that are visually bright, or brighter than your companions. They will be loving too, which is always a clear indication.

The second lesson is to know that there is hope, and that hell is not eternal. The Christian Churches have done mortal man a great disservice in preaching that hell is eternal. Spirits either believe this themselves, or hear it constantly from their companions. Thus it is very hard to have hope. Admittedly the environment is not conducive to hope. Imagine this:

> *It seemed as if I was standing at the top of a mountain or hill. Below I could see a pretty valley, with forests, meadows, springs and streams. I heard birds singing, it was like a beautiful summer day. Suddenly, everything began to dry off. The green colors turned brown, the leaves fell off the trees, and after a short time, I saw a disastrous landscape. Everything was dry, the earth cracked, a few trunks like skeletons without life, the streams had disappeared, leaving behind only their stony beds. There was no sunshine anymore, everything seemed dark, like a winter dawn in the northern regions, but without snow, and the silence of death reigned.[12]*

Let's assume you accept help. There are two types of advice that you will get. The first is basically to develop your Natural love, and to start

---

[12] www.new-birth.net/contemporary/hr21.htm received by the medium HR September 6th, 2001 in "Judas' experiences of the Hells."

helping others. One needs to repent, in the sense of accepting responsibility for where you are, and wanting to change. But most of all one needs to learn to be more loving. This as one can expect, is not easy. Particularly when those around you are not loving. While saying that this is the category of help you might get, if it was a Catholic priest offering help, you might expect him to suggest you follow his faith. The extent, to which this sort of narrow religious advice is given, really depends on the level of the spirit offering the advice. The more advanced spirits do realize that many conventional religions have much the same effect, and that therefore love is the common denominator. But lower down, most spirits cling tenaciously to their religious beliefs. So you may get a lot of pastors, all favouring their brand of religion, trying to help you. But there are also many organized groups of people, who do not ascribe to any specific religious belief, who offer help to those in the dark planes. They typically have names like: "The Brotherhood of Hope".

The reason why this process is so slow is that we are as we think. Amazingly, thoughts have been described as real, and as having a real existence in this realm. We have to change our thoughts in order to change, and that can be hard.

The second category of advice that you might receive introduces a totally new concept. Here you will be told that if you pray from the heart (soul) to God and ask for His Divine Love, you will feel this Love. It may take a few days, or a week, but you will feel this Love as a real sensation. If you keep on asking, each time you will receive a small portion of Divine Love. This Love is a physical reality, and will purify your soul. This is the short cut method. Not only does it get you out of darkness faster than any other way, but also it will accelerate your spiritual progress through the heavens. Many dark spirits have attested to its effectiveness, but they also caution how hard it is to think of spiritual things while in hell. Of course since almost nobody has heard of this short cut method, they may dismiss it out of hand. But since it promises almost instant results, I suggest it is well worth trying. You don't have anything to lose.

This technique also works on earth. That is to say, you can feel the Love, and you will notice yourself changing over the next year or so. And we have had confirmation that humans following this method are in general much brighter in their spirit body than the general mortal population. It does something at a very fundamental level.

THE FIRST SPHERE.

Hell is of course in the first sphere, but most of us would not consider the upper reaches of the First Sphere as being in darkness. That is because we are used to earth, a planet that is itself largely in darkness. Above "hell" one finds the "Twilight Zone", and then "Summerland". These are spiritualist terms. Some spiritualists teach that Summerland is the Third Sphere, but that is apparently not so, they are simply numbering sub-spheres as major spheres.

In the upper reaches of the first sphere, spirits use tools to create things, just like here. Later on, this is unnecessary because they learn how to use their minds instead. They live in homes, and learn how to manipulate their spirit bodies. They can for example have a perfect physique, or a full head of hair. Most spirits choose a physical form from somewhere between twenty and thirty, one which I guess represents their physical prime.

Here the spirits find that their desires result in changes to their spirit bodies. So, although they do not initially have conscious control over this aspect, they do look attractive, with perfect bodies. In time these "material" pleasures pall, and the spirit finds itself drawn more to spiritual avenues, and that this gives it increased happiness. At that stage they are then starting to progress out of this sphere.

They also discover making love in the spirit is a bit different, and very enjoyable. It is accomplished by a sort of fusion of energy between the souls. Having been fortunate enough to experience it a few times, in out of body experiences, I can report that it is indeed something to look forward to. Homes are provided too. The way in which buildings and other created items are made is intriguing, and explained by Monsignor

Robert Hugh Benson[13]. Apparently you can decorate or change your home. Folks specialize in all these activities, including for example making flowers. The flowers are eternal in nature, and responsive. I rather suspect we will not have an autumn in heaven, and that slightly saddens me. There is no decay, so I can't see how one achieves the magic show of autumn leaves that we have here on earth. Of course one could create an unchanging autumn show, but that would not be quite the same.

Even the homes in the upper planes of the First Sphere are very comfortable, allowing for the fact that they don't have kitchens or bathrooms, but later on they seem to be better than the grandest mansion one might imagine. In hell they are hovels or caves, although apparently many cities also exist there. The old Bible phrase – "in my Father's house are many mansions" has more than a ring of Truth. But the weather is so benevolent, that if you did not want to live in a house, you could entirely do without one.

Animals and pets are found in spirit. There is no doubt at all, if you have a much loved cat, dog or even elephant, that you will enjoy its companionship again. It is not the case that all animals automatically survive death, but much loved ones are found again. It is likely that this is a creation emanating from the love that we hold for that animal. On the other hand, apparently there are places in the spirit world where you can go and see the dinosaurs, so no doubt all manner of animal can be found, for our enjoyment. Of course many pets pass over before us, and thus someone will be looking after them there.

Strangely many spirits report feeling cold when they first arrive, but later this is not a problem. It is quite widely accepted that spirits are cold when they appear in our realm, and at least one spirit has reported being able to feel the heat from a fire in our realm, as well as clearly hearing sound from our realm.

---

[13] "Life in the World Unseen" by Anthony Borgia.

Spirits spend a great deal of time discussing God. Does He exist etc. Naturally religious groups exist, and spirits will follow those beliefs by attending church etc. Spiritual ignorance abounds, as one would expect. That does not mean spirits are un-opinionated. Indeed it seems some of the most opinionated spirits can be found in the first and Second Spheres. The old adage of the empty can making the most noise seems true of spirit as well. Arguments are even more intense than on earth. This is because each spirit will now have some experiences that support their belief.

The level of ignorance is actually very high, but that does not stop many spirits attending séances and coming through with a great deal of misplaced authority. These are the spirits who may use Jesus' name, or even call themselves God. One also finds spirits here who are mischievous, and immature, rather than evil. They will also delight in frightening mortals at séances.

Summerland has been described as having a climate similar to California. But without the pollution! There are a great number of children in Summerland, but they are not found lower, which is quite reasonable. The landscape is beautiful, with pretty villages and cities. Spirits can choose to live in a city, or in the country. I may finally get that water view I always wanted! The cities don't have roads, indeed there are no roads anywhere, and typically the height of the buildings is limited to a few stories. So the typical landscape of a city would be quite different to what we might be used to, with no pavements or tables on sidewalks. But the grander buildings have large paved areas, and patio areas.

There is still a degree of negativity, which is illustrated by gossip, differences of opinion, and anger. But most spirits are pretty used to that from earth, and probably don't really notice it. Sports are indulged, but there are issues playing ball sports. Apparently the gravity is quite different, and to launch a ball one needs to use thought power. Once so launched, it will not stop until redirected again by thought. So sending a ball towards the goal would always reach the goal, and rather seems to make sports such as football and golf irrelevant. That might hugely upset some folks, so I hope there is something as addictive for the golfing fraternity. I was very pleased to discover one can have a boat, if one has the development, and that this can be "motorised" by thought. It is even possible to sail, but as the winds are very gentle, I guess it is again largely thought powered.

It is here in the First Sphere that spirits tend to discover what they really want to do, and what talents they have. As they don't have to work, and there is no authority chasing them, they are totally free to devote whatever time they like to pursuits. Spirits find that they can follow material pursuits here, but in time the attractiveness of that fades, and suddenly they begin to realize that spirituality is important, and a greater source of happiness.

THE SECOND SPHERE.

The essential requirement for a spirit to reach the Second Sphere is the recognition that material pursuits are limited, and do not lead to real happiness. In the second sphere, spirits choose their spiritual path. These are by no means uniform, and in general, if a spirit decides later to change to another spiritual path, they will return to this sphere.

In fact there are two great classifications of spiritual path, but this distinction is probably not obvious to most spirits. The first classification is the Natural Love path. In this class, one finds all the religions, and even those following an intellectual, and non-religious path. Many people have remarked that love is the basis of most religions, but the love they are referring to is the Natural love. Slowly but surely, spirits become more loving, and advance steadily through the spheres, stopping at the sixth, but generally bypassing the Third and Fifth. The Sixth is a heaven of complete happiness, so complete that spirits lack nothing, and cannot envisage anything better.

The second classification is the Divine Love path. If you took the short cut out of hell, you will have found so much happiness flowing into your soul, that this will be the path you will follow. Not many spirits follow this path however.

In this Second Sphere, which can be called a sphere of decision, it is really like a kindergarten. In the first spheres, many things were built by machine. Here in the second, spirits are learning to use their spirit powers, assisted by other more advanced spirits. There are many institutions of learning, and this sphere is well known to many spiritualists.

They learn to modify their clothes, to build their houses using spiritual power, and to even modify aspects of their spiritual bodies. This exposure to the spiritual powers that are available generates a state of euphoria, and as a result many spirits stay here a long time. It is such fun. That is no bad thing; there is no timetable to keep.

In deciding what development path to follow, spirits are influenced by those from more advanced spheres. Thus a spirit from the Fourth Sphere may well extol the virtues of his path, and the beauty of his sphere. Spirits in many cases retain some of the spiritual ideas they had in the first sphere, but they may be beginning to modify those to some extent. Some of them have a period of confusion, for example if they believe that they should now stand before God, or perhaps Jesus. As that does not happen, it takes a while to rationalize, and evolve a new spiritual or religious strategy.

Jesus does visit these spirits, but they do not generally recognize him. He cannot display himself as he really is, because his spiritual brightness is far too powerful to be revealed in these lower spheres, and hence they generally do not accord him any special status. We have been told that the sun is like a candle compared to his spiritual brightness. All more advanced spirits have to limit the brightness they display in the lower levels.

The Second Sphere is a real heaven, as it has immense facilities for study, facilities that cannot be dreamed of on earth. Eventually however, each and every spirit eventually arrives at the highest plane in this sphere. There a tremendous change occurs. They remember that they have got this far through the help given them by numerous spirits, and a great urge overtakes them to perform a similar function. It is an atonement task.

THE THIRD SPHERE.

Spirits in the Third Sphere have both sufficient love, and spiritual understanding to begin to perform a useful task of helping other spirits. Because of their greater spiritual development, they can also begin to perceive the Will of God, although this is not because they can perceive God.

Typically the tasks that they undertake have something to do with their earth life. I came across a fellow getting a lot of help from an ex-playgirl. This fellow had very strong sexual desires, and she was trying very hard to influence him away from those. Clearly she had to atone for inciting so many fellows to sexual desires by being a playgirl. Another may be a pastor, who has spent a lifetime spreading false doctrines. He may find himself trying to undo those false beliefs. This work can be very hard, and these spirits do experience frustration. However this does not mean that all these spirits are teaching only truth. These spirits still have many of their earth beliefs, provided always that none of these are seriously harmful from a spiritual perspective. Where that is the case, they do not progress, until they come to a realisation that their belief is false.

Those spirits following the Divine Love path may spend a long time in this sphere, because they feel the importance of the task of teaching this "new" Truth. As they also do not find the Fourth Sphere particularly congenial, they would generally stay here till they can reach the Fifth. When finally what started out as a work of atonement, and now becomes a vocational choice, the spirit is ready to move on.

Here is a description of a home in the Third Sphere:

Yes, my home is very beautiful and I am perfectly delighted with it. It is made of white marble and is surrounded by lawns and flowers and trees of various kinds. The grass is so very green and the flowers are so beautiful and variegated. The trees are always in foliage and have such beautiful limbs and leaves. I am most pleased with my home, I mean the building. There are many beautiful pictures on the walls, and the walls are all frescoed and hung with fine coverings, and the floors are inlaid with beautiful mosaics. I have all the splendid furniture that I could possibly wish for, and my library is full of books of all kinds, especially of those that tell of God and His Love for man. You would be in your element if you could be with me.

I have music, such as you never heard on earth, and instruments of various kinds which I am learning to play, and I sing with all my heart and soul as the days go by. I have beds on which I lie down, but I never sleep. We do not need sleep here; we only rest, for sometimes we get tired from our work and are greatly refreshed by lying on the beds and couches which are so comfortable that we do not realize that we are tired after lying down a little while.[14]

---

[14] www.new-birth.net/tgrabjvol2/heaven7.htm received by James Padgett on November 30th, 1914

THE FOURTH SPHERE.

The spirits in this sphere are now used as teachers in the various learning institutions, and they develop in this sphere their sometimes astonishing healing abilities. It is largely an intellectual sphere, and some spirits following a Divine Love path spend almost no time here, moving virtually directly on to the Fifth Sphere once they are able. Others chose to stay here, although they can do much the same work in the Fifth Sphere. There is beginning to be a bigger and bigger difference between spirits following the Natural Love and the intellectual path, and those following the Divine Love path.

Earthly bonds weaken, and spirits are not much interested in the affairs of earth. Even familial bonds weaken. This does not mean that they do not care for other members of their genetic families, but their general love for all mankind is now so strong, that familial love recedes in contrast.

Soul mates now begin to be a topic of great interest. It is true we all have a soul mate. This is because the initial creation of souls creates pairs of souls. This appears to be yet another technique that God has provided to gather his creation closer. Inevitably one soul mate will be more advanced. Their great love for each other spurs the less developed one to make great efforts to catch up, so that they can live together. Sometimes this is in fact the way a soul is "extracted" from the hells. The more advanced soul mate is able to influence the less developed one to make the effort to get out of darkness. What is intriguing is that this soul mate attraction is so strong that a bright and pure spirit is actually attracted at all to a dark spirit.

The Fourth Sphere, with its great facilities is often a sphere where spirits stay a very long time. By the time that these spirits have reached the upper planes of this sphere, they will have all but lost interest in the affairs of mortal man. Their only interest is in helping man to progress, but they take no personal interest in his affairs.

THE FIFTH SPHERE.

This is what is termed a soul sphere, and those spirits following a Natural Love path do not spend much time here. But it is an important sphere for Divine Love spirits. The only thing that Natural Love spirits lack is absolute purity. They must eradicate the last traces of sin. They may still cling to false beliefs, but none of these will be harmful. This last stage of purification does not take long, and the Natural Love spirits then progress into the sixth, the ultimate goal of their spiritual path.

There is no reason for them to tarry here, since there is more happiness to be had in the sixth. There is also little commonality between them and Divine love spirits. They have a fundamentally different belief, and spiritual path, and this leads to different interests.

In fact many of the Divine Love spirits also hasten to enter the sixth, and then return. The sixth is not entirely congenial to them, and they have much development that they can do in the Fifth. And, once they have received more of the Divine Love, they can progress directly to the Seventh Sphere.

It was reported that Mother Teresa passed over into the Fifth Sphere, and that is the highest that we have heard of for a mortal, although there have been others. Just recently we heard that Francis of Assisi also passed into the Fifth. Few could doubt the love that Mother Teresa had, or the spiritual fervour that Francis of Assisi had. Dr Stone, who assisted James Padgett[15] with his spiritual revelations also passed into the Fifth. What is interesting is neither Mother Teresa nor Francis of Assisi would have been schooled in the concept of Divine Love, yet their spiritual fervour was such that they followed this path

---

[15] The Padgett Messages published at www.new-birth.net

automatically. It is in fact possible to find this path intuitively, and is probably something that has distinguished many of the "saints".

Here is a description of a home in the Fifth Sphere:

I am living with your mother in her home, but I am not so spiritual as she. We are both very happy though, and have everything that the heart could wish for. The music is so beautiful that I cannot describe it to you, and even the love which helps to make the music is of such an intensity that you could not possibly understand if I should attempt to tell it to you. My home here is much more beautiful than that which I had in the third sphere, and everything is beyond what I conceived when I lived there. The house and trees and flowers and fruits are very much more beautiful and delightful.

No one could be anything but happy in such a home. We have nothing to interfere with our happiness and every one is a delightful companion and full of love and beauty. I have met many spirits that I did not know either on earth or in the spirit world before I came to this place, both men and women.

Yes, we have rivers and lakes and fields and mountains and all the beautiful landscapes that you can imagine, I not only enjoy these things, but they are more real than those of earth. I am sometimes engaged in painting these flowers and landscapes, and have many pictures which others painted. I find that I can paint with a more artistic touch than when on earth. I have no trouble in drawing as you know I had some in my earth pictures. I am also studying music, and especially my vocal lessons. You will be much surprised when you hear me sing as you cannot conceive what a different voice I have. Sometimes I try to sing some of the songs that I used to sing to you, but they are not pretty in comparison to the songs we have here, either in the music or the sentiments.[16]

---

[16] www.new-birth.net/tgrabjvol3/heaven8.htm received by James Padgett on January 7th 1915

THE SIXTH SPHERE.

This is the pinnacle of spiritual development for Natural Love spirits. It represents a return to the Adamic state. However, they quite possibly would dispute that there are any higher spheres. Certainly Divine Love spirits find that these spirits are not interested in listening to this concept. They enjoy themselves with many very advanced intellectual and moral discussions. One should realize that mental capacity has expanded enormously along with spiritual development. This is a perfect heaven, and spirits lack for nothing, and cannot imagine anything better could exist.

The Sixth Sphere is a purely intellectual area, and by that I mean that in spite of the great spirituality of the place, the zeal of its inhabitants goes much more for increasing their knowledge, while they live a life in absolute harmony with God's laws of spirituality. It is a place where science has reached its most spectacular results compared to all the spiritual spheres, and where the intelligence of its inhabitants is supreme, and where absolute fraternity exists, such as people dream of on earth. There are great social events, amusements, all of which provides them with great happiness, their class of happiness. Paradise, yes, the Sixth Sphere is the Paradise which the Hebrews dreamt of and continue dreaming of, and it is the Paradise that Christian churches teach of, and also spiritualists.

Religion is important too, and there is a great diversity of religious practice. That indicates that the inhabitants are not in possession of absolute truth. It is rare for these spirits to communicate with mortals. But many work as teachers and professors in lower spheres.

Divine Love spirits can enter this sphere, but generally do not stay long. They simply find that their interests are different. So they return to the Fifth until they are able to pass into the Seventh.

As these Sixth Sphere spirits do not progress any further, it is not known what their long-term future will be. Some sources suggest eventually all will awaken to the fact that something is lacking – God's Divine Love, and progress will then resume. Other sources suggest that in fact the "second death" will mean that these spirits are isolated, and the "gates" to the Kingdom of God will be closed, leaving them excluded. Another revelation[17] suggests their future will lie in the local universe in which the earth lies, rather than being able to reach other parts of this universe, or the Central Paradise where Father resides, or even other universes.

---

[17] The Urantia Book

THE SEVENTH SPHERE.

This sphere is only populated by Divine Love spirits. It marks the beginning of a series of changes that will eventually leave them quite different to other spirits. So different, that it is said they cannot be considered to be of the same family. The first change is that the soul manifests a mind, which is different to the material mind that all other spirits utilize. This begins to dominate. Eventually, before the spirit leaves this sphere, the material mind of the spirit body will have entirely withered away, leaving the spirit using the mind of the soul. (There is a different perspective on this, that rather than "growing" a soul mind, we actually start to access the Divine mind of our Indwelling Spirit.)

The duration of the process of the last stage of transformation varies. It may be achieved in a relatively short time, but many spirits stay longer in this wonderful paradise, enjoying and experiencing, like tourists taking their time to explore the last corner of their unknown world.

They gain enormous knowledge in this sphere, in this process, and without study. The knowledge simply comes to them. Eventually they are ready for the transition. In the transition to the Celestial heavens which lie above the Seventh Sphere, they fuse with their Indwelling Spirit, or Thought Adjuster[18] which has accompanied them since their earliest years. This gives the Indwelling Spirit personality and the spirit gains Divinity and immortality. Spirits who have passed this stage tell us they know they are immortal. There is no debate, such as exists in the Sixth Sphere. They then become spiritual beings, as opposed to semi-material beings. This difference must be subtle, because other less developed spirits do not seem able to discern the difference. Or

---

[18] The name used in The Urantia Book.

perhaps it's simply the fact that when an advanced spirit visits lower spheres, they find that they take on more of the "hues" of those levels, and thus the difference is not great at that level.

There are "un-numbered" spheres in the Celestial Heavens above, each more magnificent than the rest. Spirits who reside here complain that words simply cannot describe these spheres, and generally they just won't try. These would appear to be the classic **Kingdom of God** that the Christian Bible talks about. But this concludes our summary. Ironically, because this is probably only the start of our next adventure, the re-birth by spirit that the Christian Bible promises to those who have faith that Father loves us. And an eternity of growth and spiritual adventure lies ahead. Perhaps there will be another narrow path we might have to navigate beyond the Kingdom of God? A particularly good video of this long journey to Paradise, based on the Urantia book, can be found on this web site: http://www.squarecircles.com/

Originally Created 21st April 2003, Current Revision: 6.5: 11th May 2012.

Sources:

Most of these sources are available with free e-books, or are freely available on the internet in text form. The www.new-birth.net web site hosts many of these references, as well as other intriguing spiritual books.

"True Gospel Revealed Anew by Jesus", Volumes I to IV. These are also referred to as The Padgett Messages.

Contemporary spirit communications on www.new-birth.net

"Life in the World Unseen", by Anthony Borgia

"More About Life in the World Unseen" by Anthony Borgia

"Here and Hereafter" by Anthony Borgia

"Through the Mists" by Robert James Lees

"The Life Elysian" by Robert James Lees

"The Gate of Heaven" by Robert James Lees

"Spirit World and Spirit Life" by Charlotte Elizabeth Dresser

"Life Here and Hereafter" by Charlotte Elizabeth Dresser

"The Blue Island" by Pardoe Woodman and Estelle Stead

"30 Years among the Dead" by Dr Carl Wickland

"A Wanderer in the Spirit Lands" by Franchezzo.

"Gone West" by J.S.M Ward

"A Sequel to Gone West: A Subaltern in Spirit Land" by J.S.M. Ward

The Urantia Book published by The Urantia Foundation.

"More Alive Than Ever... Always Karen" by Jeanne Walker